GOLD COAST

Travel Guide 2024

Lovely Things to Do in the Glitter Strip; Tips, Tricks and Recommendations for Every Traveler

Betty Vanslyke

Copyright © 2024 by Betty Vanslyke

All rights reserved. No part of this publication may be reproduced, distributed, or transmitted in any form or by any means, including photocopying, recording, or other electronic or mechanical methods, without the prior written permission of the publisher, except in the case of brief quotations embodied in critical reviews and certain other noncommercial uses permitted by copyright law.

TABLE OF CONTENT

TABLE OF CONTENT 2

MAP OF GOLD COAST 6

INTRODUCTION 7

    Discovering the Gold Coast 7

    Echoes of Time - Gold Coast's History and Cultural Tapestry 9

CHAPTER ONE 12

    Getting Started 12

        Crafting Your Gold Coast Adventure - Trip Planning Unveiled 12

        Navigating the Gold Coast - Your Transportation Odyssey 14

CHAPTER TWO 16

    Beach Bliss 16

        Sands of Bliss - Exploring the Gold Coast's Coastal Gems 16

        Aqua Adventures - Diving into Gold Coast's Water Wonderland 18

        Sunset Vibes - Beachfront Dining and Nightlife Extravaganza 20

CHAPTER THREE 22

    Theme Park Extravaganza 22

        Thrills and Wonders - Profiles of Gold Coast's Major Theme Parks ... 22

        Mastering the Gold Coast - Tips for Maximizing Your Visit 24

CHAPTER FOUR 27

Natural Wonders 27

Nature's Symphony - Exploring Gold Coast's National Parks and Reserves 27

Hiker's Haven - Exploring Gold Coast's Hiking and Outdoor Activities 29

CHAPTER FIVE 32

Cityscape Exploration 32

Cityscape Chronicles - Touring Gold Coast's Landmarks 32

Retail Revelry - Exploring Gold Coast's Shopping Districts and Markets 34

CHAPTER SIX 37

Culinary Delights 37

Culinary Chronicles - Indulging in Gold Coast's Local Cuisine Highlights 37

Culinary Gems - Recommended Restaurants and Cafés 39

CHAPTER SEVEN 45

Nightlife and Entertainment 45

Nightlife Revelry - Bars, Clubs, and Entertainment Venues 45

Festival Frenzy - Gold Coast's Events and Festivals 47

CHAPTER EIGHT 50

Family-Friendly Fun 50

Family Fun - Kid-Friendly Attractions on the Gold Coast 50

Bonding Beyond the Beach - Family-Oriented Activities on the Gold Coast 52

GOLD COAST

CHAPTER NINE 55

Adventure Seekers 55

Adrenaline Unleashed - Extreme Sports and Adrenaline Activities.... 55

Into the Wild - Outdoor Adventure Recommendations on the Gold Coast 57

CHAPTER TEN 60

Cultural Immersion 60

Cultural Odyssey - Museums and Art Galleries on the Gold Coast..... 60

Cultural Revelry - Gold Coast's Cultural Events and Festivals............ 62

CHAPTER ELEVEN 65

Gold Coast Tours 65

Conquering the Gold Coast: A Tour Guide for Every Traveler 65

Nature's Embrace: Rainforest Delights.. 65

Thrills & Spills: Adrenaline Adventures 66

Wildlife Encounters: Unforgettable Connections................................. 67

Cultural Immersion: Local Gems.. 68

CHAPTER TWELVE 71

Accommodation Guide 71

Stay and Play - Overview of Different Areas to Stay on the Gold Coast 71

Coastal Comforts - Recommendations for Various Budgets on the Gold Coast 73

CHAPTER THIRTEEN 92

Practical Tips..92

    Cultural Courtesies - Local Customs and Etiquette on the Gold Coast 92

    Safe and Sound - Safety and Health Information on the Gold Coast . 95

CHAPTER FOURTEEN... 99

Gold Coast Toolkit..99

    Navigating the Coast - Maps and Useful Contacts on the Gold Coast 99

    Map of Surfers Paradise 100

    Map of Broadbeach 101

    Map of Surfers Paradise 102

    Map of Tamborine Mountain 103

    Map of Palm Beach.. 104

    Map of Q1 Skypoint Observation Deck 105

CONCLUSION *108*

MAP OF GOLD COAST

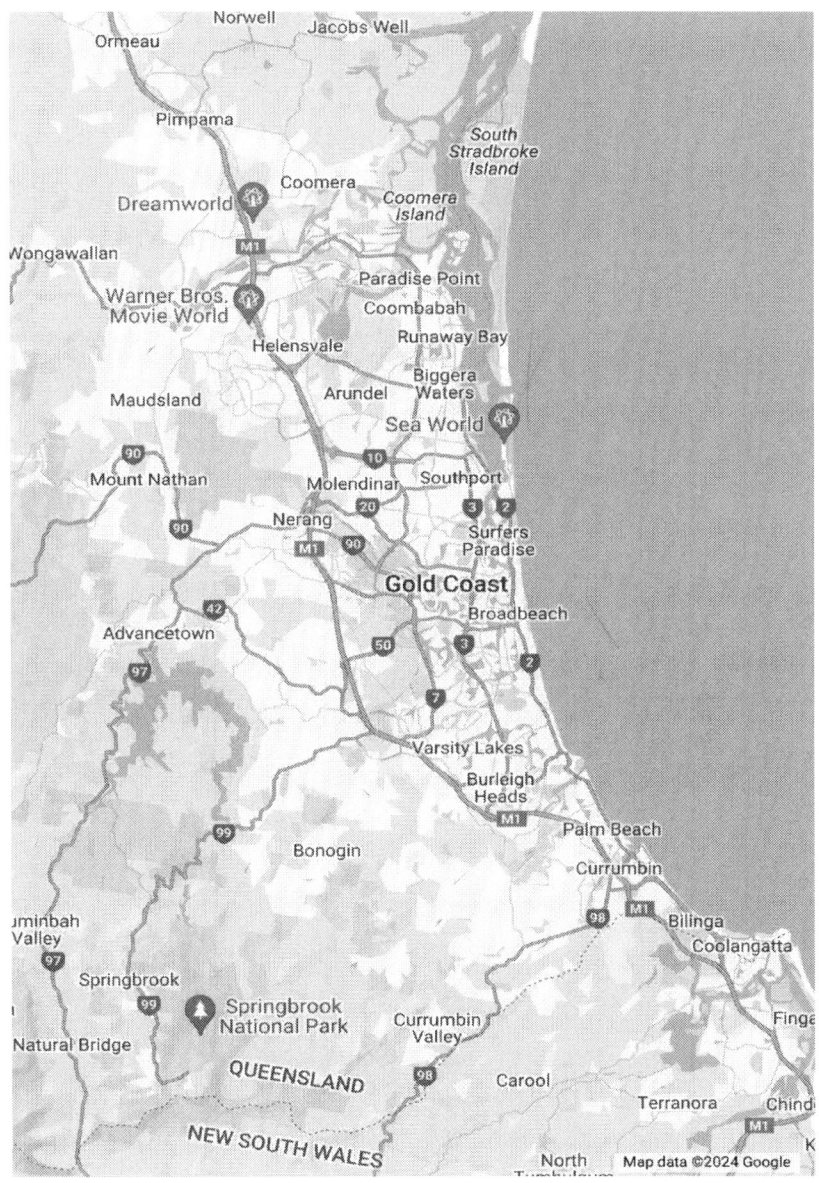

INTRODUCTION

Discovering the Gold Coast

Welcome to the vibrant and sun-kissed paradise that is the Gold Coast! Nestled along the southeastern coast of Queensland, Australia, the Gold Coast beckons with a magnetic charm, seamlessly blending pristine beaches,

thrilling adventures, and a rich tapestry of culture. In this chapter, we embark on a journey to unravel the essence of this coastal gem.

Unlock the secrets of the Gold Coast:

- **A Playground of Sunshine:** Bask in the year-round sunshine that graces the Gold Coast, making it a haven for beach enthusiasts and outdoor adventurers alike.

- **Golden Sands and Azure Waters:** Explore the picturesque beaches that have become synonymous with the region. From the iconic Surfers Paradise to the tranquil Burleigh Heads, each stretch of sand tells its own story.

- **Thrills Beyond the Shore:** Dive into the heart-pounding excitement of theme parks that define the Gold Coast experience. Get ready for a roller coaster ride of adrenaline and family-friendly fun.

- **Surf, Sand, and Skyline:** Immerse yourself in the dynamic cityscape, where modern architecture meets the laid-back coastal lifestyle. Discover the perfect blend of urban sophistication and natural beauty.

As we embark on this exploration, let the allure of the Gold Coast captivate your senses, promising an unforgettable journey filled with sunsets over the Pacific, laughter echoing through theme park rides, and the warm embrace of a destination that invites you to create your own story in the golden embrace of Australia's beloved coastline.

Echoes of Time - Gold Coast's History and Cultural Tapestry

Unveiling the Rich Tapestry:

Delve into the intriguing history and vibrant cultural background that shape the Gold Coast into the captivating destination it is today.

Unearthing the Past: Explore the indigenous roots that date back thousands of years, discovering the deep connection of the Yugambeh and Kombumerri peoples to this land. Uncover tales of trade routes, ancient ceremonies, and the harmony between humans and nature.

Colonial Footprints: Trace the footsteps of European explorers and settlers, witnessing the transformation of the Gold Coast from a quiet hinterland into a bustling region during the 19th century. Learn about the impact of the gold rush and the birth of early communities.

Surf, Sand, and Hollywood Glamour: Witness the post-war boom that turned the Gold Coast into a glittering coastal playground. From the glamorous days of Hollywood films to the rise of tourism, understand how

GOLD COAST

this paradise evolved into a global destination for sun-seekers and thrill-seekers alike.

A Cultural Mosaic: Immerse yourself in the cultural diversity that defines the Gold Coast today. From international festivals to a burgeoning arts scene, discover how this coastal haven embraces a melting pot of influences, creating a unique and inclusive atmosphere.

Embark on a historical and cultural odyssey, where the echoes of time resonate through the streets, beaches, and hinterlands of the Gold Coast. This chapter sets the stage, inviting you to appreciate the layers of heritage that contribute to the region's dynamic and ever-evolving identity.

CHAPTER ONE

Getting Started

Crafting Your Gold Coast Adventure - Trip Planning Unveiled

Turning Dreams into Reality:

Embark on a journey of meticulous planning as we unravel the secrets to creating your perfect Gold Coast getaway.

Setting the Stage: Begin with an overview of the best times to visit, taking into account weather, events, and seasonal attractions. Whether you crave the buzz of summer festivals or the tranquility of a winter escape, find the ideal timeframe for your adventure.

Navigating the Gold Coast Map: Explore the geography of the region, breaking down key areas and their unique offerings. From the bustling Surfers Paradise to the secluded beauty of Currumbin, understand the distinct personalities each locale brings to the table.

Crafting Your Itinerary: Dive into the plethora of activities the Gold Coast has to offer. Tailor your itinerary to your interests, whether it's sun-soaked beach days, heart-pounding theme park adventures, or cultural explorations. Discover insider tips to maximize your time and make every moment count.

Accommodation Alchemy: Navigate the diverse range of accommodations, from luxurious beachfront resorts to budget-friendly hostels. Find the perfect home base for your Gold Coast escapade, ensuring comfort, convenience, and a touch of local charm.

Practicalities Unveiled: Equip yourself with essential travel tips, from currency exchange to transportation options. Uncover the nuances of local etiquette and customs, ensuring a smooth and enjoyable experience as you immerse yourself in the Gold Coast way of life.

With this section as your guide, transform your travel aspirations into a well-crafted plan, setting the stage for a Gold Coast adventure that aligns perfectly with your desires and expectations. Get ready to embrace the excitement of planning and anticipate the unforgettable moments that await you in this coastal paradise.

Navigating the Gold Coast - Your Transportation Odyssey

Seamless Journeys Await:

Embark on a comprehensive exploration of the transportation options that will whisk you effortlessly through the captivating landscapes of the Gold Coast.

Highways and Byways: Discover the scenic routes and major highways that connect the Gold Coast's diverse locales. From the iconic Pacific Motorway to charming coastal drives, navigate the roads with confidence, allowing the journey itself to become an integral part of your adventure.

Public Transport Symphony: Dive into the efficiency and convenience of the Gold Coast's public transportation network. Uncover the secrets of the G:link light rail system, buses, and ferries, ensuring you can effortlessly explore the city and its surroundings while taking in breathtaking views along the way.

Rental Car Freedom: For those craving flexibility, unravel the perks of renting a car. Whether you're venturing into the lush hinterlands or exploring hidden beaches, having your own wheels opens up a world of possibilities.

Sky-High Marvels: Elevate your experience with insights into air travel options. Uncover the convenience of Gold Coast Airport, providing a gateway to the region for domestic and international travelers. Explore tips for a smooth arrival and departure, setting the tone for a seamless journey.

Navigating by Foot and Bike: For the eco-conscious explorer, delve into pedestrian-friendly areas and bike paths. Embrace the charm of strolling through vibrant neighborhoods or cycling along the picturesque coastline, immersing yourself in the Gold Coast's natural beauty.

This section serves as your transportation compass, guiding you through the myriad options available to ensure your journey across the Gold Coast is not only efficient but also a delightful adventure in itself. Get ready to traverse this coastal paradise with ease and excitement.

CHAPTER TWO

Beach Bliss

Sands of Bliss - Exploring the Gold Coast's Coastal Gems

Where Sun Meets Surf:

Immerse yourself in the quintessential allure of the Gold Coast as we unfold the golden pages of its breathtaking beaches, each a unique testament to the coastal paradise's beauty.

1. Surfers Paradise Beach: Embark on a journey to the iconic Surfers Paradise, where golden sands meet the vibrant energy of the city. Dive into the surf culture, explore the bustling esplanade, and witness the skyline transform with the hues of a mesmerizing sunset.

2. Burleigh Heads Beach: Discover the laid-back charm of Burleigh Heads, where nature and surf collide. Explore the headland, dotted with ancient pandanus trees, and feel the rhythm of the ocean as you stroll along the pristine beach, embraced by a relaxed atmosphere.

3. Coolangatta and Greenmount Beach: Delve into the southern charm of Coolangatta and Greenmount Beach, where rolling waves meet a more tranquil ambiance. Experience the allure of the Twin Towns and relish the panoramic views from Point Danger.

4. Main Beach: Uncover the sophistication of Main Beach, where luxury resorts and upscale dining complement the golden coastline. Whether you're indulging in watersports or enjoying a seaside meal, Main Beach offers a refined escape.

5. Currumbin Beach: Journey to Currumbin, where the beach meets the serenity of the Currumbin Creek. Explore the renowned Alley for a surfer's paradise or partake in the unique experience of feeding the friendly lorikeets at Currumbin Wildlife Sanctuary.

Explore the diversity of the Gold Coast's beaches, each a sandy canvas with its own personality. From the vibrant energy of Surfers Paradise to the tranquility of Currumbin, let the waves guide you through an unforgettable coastal journey.

Aqua Adventures - Diving into Gold Coast's Water Wonderland

Immersive Thrills Await:

Dive into the aquatic playground that the Gold Coast offers, where turquoise waters beckon thrill-seekers and water enthusiasts alike. This chapter unveils a spectrum of water activities to turn your coastal escape into an unforgettable adventure.

1. Surfing Sensations: Ride the waves of the Pacific Ocean with insights into the best surf spots for every skill level. Whether you're a seasoned surfer chasing barrels or a beginner catching your first break, the Gold Coast's beaches offer the perfect canvas for an exhilarating surfing experience.

2. Paddleboarding Paradise: Embark on a serene journey atop a paddleboard, gliding over the crystal-clear waters of the Gold Coast. From the peaceful estuaries to the open sea, discover the scenic beauty that unfolds when you stand-up paddleboard through hidden waterways.

3. Scuba Diving Depths: Plunge into the underwater wonders of the Gold Coast with a guide to scuba diving hotspots. Explore vibrant coral reefs, encounter marine life, and unveil the hidden treasures that lie beneath the surface of the Pacific.

4. Jet Skiing Adventures: Feel the rush of adrenaline as you zip across the ocean on a jet ski. Navigate through the waves and experience the thrill of high-speed water adventures, all while enjoying panoramic views of the coastline.

5. Whale Watching Spectacle: Embark on a majestic journey to witness the annual migration of humpback whales. From specially equipped boats, marvel at these gentle giants breaching and playing in their natural habitat, creating an awe-inspiring connection with the marine world.

Whether you seek the excitement of surfing, the tranquility of paddleboarding, or the mesmerizing beauty of underwater realms, the Gold Coast's aquatic wonders promise a spectrum of experiences for water enthusiasts of all kinds. Get ready to make a splash and embrace the vibrant coastal lifestyle.

Sunset Vibes - Beachfront Dining and Nightlife Extravaganza

Savoring the Coastal Nights:

As the sun dips below the horizon, the Gold Coast transforms into a vibrant tapestry of beachfront dining and nightlife. This chapter unveils the best spots to relish exquisite cuisine, sip on crafted cocktails, and dance the night away with the sound of crashing waves as your soundtrack.

1. Seaside Gastronomy: Indulge your senses in beachfront dining delights as we guide you to the most exquisite restaurants overlooking the ocean. From fresh seafood feasts to international culinary journeys, each seaside venue promises a gastronomic experience that mirrors the beauty of the coastal backdrop.

2. Oceanfront Bars and Lounges: Sip on handcrafted cocktails and savor the coastal breeze at the Gold Coast's chic oceanfront bars and lounges. Uncover hidden gems where mixologists create masterpieces, and each sip is a celebration of the seaside atmosphere.

3. Night Markets by the Shore: Explore the lively night markets that come alive along the beachfront. Immerse yourself in the festive ambiance, indulge in street food delicacies, and shop for unique treasures as the coastline transforms into a vibrant nocturnal marketplace.

4. Beach Bonfires and Moonlit Events: Discover the magic of beach bonfires and moonlit events that create an enchanting atmosphere along the shoreline. From fire-dancing performances to moonlit yoga sessions, experience the Gold Coast's nightlife in unique and captivating ways.

5. Dance under the Stars: Embark on a journey through the Gold Coast's vibrant nightlife. From beachfront clubs to open-air dance floors, let the rhythm of the night guide you as you dance under the stars, surrounded by the energy of the coastal nightlife scene.

Savor the allure of the Gold Coast after dark, where beachfront dining and nightlife converge to create an atmosphere of culinary delights, vibrant energy, and unforgettable moments by the water's edge. Get ready to indulge in a coastal nightlife experience like no other.

CHAPTER THREE

Theme Park Extravaganza

Thrills and Wonders - Profiles of Gold Coast's Major Theme Parks

Unlocking the Gates of Excitement:

Embark on an adrenaline-fueled journey as we unravel the enchanting worlds within the major theme parks that define the Gold Coast's reputation as the theme park capital of Australia.

1. **Dreamworld:** Enter the realm of Dreamworld, where imagination knows no bounds. From heart-stopping rides to family-friendly attractions, explore the park's diverse zones, including the adrenaline-pumping Big 9 Thrill Rides and the enchanting DreamWorks Experience.

2. **Movie World:** Step into the magic of the silver screen at Warner Bros. Movie World. Encounter your favorite characters, experience Hollywood-inspired rides, and be dazzled by live entertainment, creating a cinematic adventure that brings the movies to life.

3. **Sea World:** Dive into the aquatic wonders of Sea World, where marine life and thrilling rides coexist. Witness captivating animal shows, embark on water-themed adventures, and explore the park's commitment to marine conservation and education.

4. **Wet'n'Wild:** Cool off in the heart of the Gold Coast at Wet'n'Wild, the ultimate water park experience. From adrenaline-pumping slides to relaxing lazy rivers, discover a water wonderland that caters to thrill-seekers and water enthusiasts of all ages.

5. **WhiteWater World:** Join the splash-filled excitement at WhiteWater World, a water park adjacent to Dreamworld. Explore exhilarating slides, wave pools, and

family-friendly attractions, creating a perfect complement to the thrills of its neighboring theme park.

Whether you seek heart-pounding thrills, magical encounters, or aquatic adventures, each park invites you to immerse yourself in a world where wonder and excitement collide. Get ready for a journey through the realms of fantasy and exhilaration that await within the gates of the Gold Coast's major theme parks.

Mastering the Gold Coast - Tips for Maximizing Your Visit

Turning Moments into Memories:

Equip yourself with insider knowledge and expert tips to ensure that your Gold Coast adventure is not just memorable but also seamlessly crafted to match your preferences and desires.

1. Early Birds Catch the Fun: Beat the crowds and make the most of your day by arriving early at popular attractions. Whether it's theme parks, beaches, or cultural sites, early mornings often offer a quieter and more immersive experience.

2. Embrace Off-Peak Adventures: Consider exploring popular spots during off-peak hours to enjoy a more relaxed atmosphere. This might include beach visits during weekdays or dining at sought-after restaurants during non-peak dining hours.

3. Invest in Multi-Day Passes: For theme park enthusiasts, consider investing in multi-day passes to maximize your experience. This allows you to explore at a leisurely pace, ensuring you don't miss any of the attractions each park has to offer.

4. Local Culinary Gems: Discover hidden culinary gems favored by locals. Venture beyond the tourist hotspots to savor authentic flavors and unique dining experiences that capture the essence of the Gold Coast's diverse food scene.

5. Plan Theme Park Strategies: Optimize your theme park visits with strategic planning. Prioritize must-see attractions, utilize express passes when available, and schedule shows and entertainment to make the most of your time.

6. Explore Beyond the Coast: While the beaches are a highlight, don't forget to explore the hinterlands and nearby towns for a different perspective. Discover charming villages, scenic lookouts, and local treasures that often escape the mainstream spotlight.

By incorporating these tips into your itinerary, you'll not only maximize your visit but also create a personalized and unforgettable experience in this coastal paradise. Get ready to elevate your Gold Coast adventure to new heights.

CHAPTER FOUR

Natural Wonders

Nature's Symphony - Exploring Gold Coast's National Parks and Reserves

Into the Wild:

Embark on a journey into the heart of nature as we unveil the hidden treasures within the national parks and reserves that grace the Gold Coast. From lush rainforests to panoramic vistas, this chapter invites you to immerse yourself in the natural wonders that define the region.

1. Lamington National Park: Step into the ancient Gondwana Rainforest at Lamington National Park. Uncover the magic of cascading waterfalls, treetop walkways, and diverse flora and fauna. Whether you're a hiking enthusiast or a nature lover seeking tranquility, Lamington offers a pristine escape.

2. Springbrook National Park: Discover the wonders of Springbrook National Park, where ancient landscapes meet contemporary beauty. Explore the Natural Bridge, marvel at the glowworm caves, and witness panoramic views from the aptly named Best of All Lookout.

3. Burleigh Head National Park: Immerse yourself in coastal beauty at Burleigh Head National Park. With walking trails offering spectacular ocean views, discover the diverse ecosystems that coexist along the coastline, creating a haven for birdwatchers and nature enthusiasts.

4. Tamborine National Park: Venture into Tamborine National Park, where rainforests, waterfalls, and walking trails beckon. Unearth the charm of Curtis Falls, meander through the botanical gardens, and indulge in the vibrant arts and crafts scene of the nearby mountain village.

5. Currumbin Wildlife Sanctuary: While not a traditional national park, Currumbin Wildlife Sanctuary deserves a mention. Encounter Australian wildlife in a natural setting, participate in interactive shows, and even feed kangaroos. This sanctuary offers a unique blend of conservation and education.

Whether you seek the ancient serenity of rainforests or the coastal beauty of headlands, the national parks and reserves of the Gold Coast promise a sanctuary for exploration and tranquility. Get ready to discover the natural symphony that awaits within these pristine landscapes.

Hiker's Haven - Exploring Gold Coast's Hiking and Outdoor Activities

Trail Tales and Adventure Awaits:

Embark on a journey through the Gold Coast's diverse landscapes, where hiking trails and outdoor activities beckon. This chapter is your guide to experiencing the region's natural beauty with exhilarating hikes and thrilling outdoor adventures.

1. Purling Brook Falls Circuit: Begin your hiking adventures with the Purling Brook Falls Circuit in Springbrook National Park. This trail takes you through lush rainforests, past stunning waterfalls, and offers breathtaking views of the Gold Coast hinterland.

2. Burleigh Head National Park Coastal Walk: Explore the coastal beauty of Burleigh Head National Park with a scenic coastal walk. Witness panoramic views of the

Pacific Ocean, spot wildlife, and enjoy the refreshing sea breeze as you traverse this picturesque trail.

3. Mount Warning Summit Track: Challenge yourself with the Mount Warning Summit Track, where the reward is a spectacular sunrise view from the highest point in the region. This iconic hike takes you through subtropical rainforest, providing a truly immersive outdoor experience.

4. Tamborine Rainforest Skywalk: For a unique perspective, take a stroll along the Tamborine Rainforest Skywalk. Elevated walkways offer a bird's-eye view of the rainforest canopy, providing a tranquil and educational experience surrounded by nature.

5. Treetop Adventures: Indulge your adventurous spirit with treetop activities. Zip-line through lush canopies, navigate high ropes courses, and experience the thrill of suspended bridges in various adventure parks across the Gold Coast.

6. Kayaking and Stand-Up Paddleboarding: Embrace the coastal lifestyle with kayaking or stand-up paddleboarding. Explore waterways, estuaries, or even venture out to the open sea, immersing yourself in the scenic beauty and serenity of the Gold Coast's aquatic landscapes.

Lace up your hiking boots and embrace the great outdoors. Whether you seek challenging summit trails, coastal strolls, or thrilling outdoor adventures, the Gold Coast offers a myriad of opportunities to connect with nature and elevate your sense of adventure. Get ready to embark on a journey of exploration and discovery in the midst of the region's stunning landscapes.

Toolona Creek Circuit

CHAPTER FIVE

Cityscape Exploration

Cityscape Chronicles - Touring Gold Coast's Landmarks

City Lights and Iconic Heights:

Embark on a captivating exploration of the Gold Coast's cityscape, where modern marvels, cultural landmarks, and iconic attractions create a dynamic urban tapestry. This chapter unveils the must-see landmarks that showcase the city's vibrant character.

1. Q1 Skypoint Observation Deck: Ascend to new heights at the Q1 Skypoint Observation Deck, offering panoramic views of the Gold Coast skyline and beyond. Witness breathtaking sunsets, take in the city lights, and gain a unique perspective on the coastal beauty that unfolds below.

2. Surfers Paradise Beachfront Markets: Immerse yourself in the lively atmosphere of the Surfers Paradise Beachfront Markets. Stroll along the iconic Esplanade, discover unique arts and crafts, and savor the eclectic flavors of the local food stalls against the backdrop of the ocean.

3. The Spit and Gold Coast Seaway: Explore the Spit, a narrow barrier between the Broadwater and the Pacific Ocean. Visit the Gold Coast Seaway for stunning views and watch as boats navigate the entrance to the Broadwater, creating a captivating maritime spectacle.

4. Skyline Circuit Walk: Embark on the Skyline Circuit Walk in Burleigh Heads, offering sweeping views of the coastline and the city. Traverse the headland and witness the juxtaposition of natural beauty and urban sophistication that defines the Gold Coast.

5. HOTA - Home of the Arts: Discover the cultural hub of the Gold Coast at HOTA - Home of the Arts. Explore contemporary art exhibitions, catch a live performance, or simply unwind in the lush outdoor spaces that blend culture and creativity.

Tour the city's landmarks, each a testament to the Gold Coast's evolution into a modern and dynamic destination. Whether you're seeking architectural marvels, cultural experiences, or vibrant markets, the cityscape of the Gold Coast promises a journey of discovery and appreciation.

Get ready to explore the iconic landmarks that shape the urban narrative of this coastal paradise.

Retail Revelry - Exploring Gold Coast's Shopping Districts and Markets

Retail Therapy and Treasures Await:

Embark on a shopping odyssey through the Gold Coast's diverse districts and markets, where boutique shops, vibrant markets, and unique finds beckon. This chapter unveils the best places to indulge in retail therapy and discover local treasures.

1. Pacific Fair Shopping Centre: Immerse yourself in retail splendor at Pacific Fair, the Gold Coast's largest shopping center. Explore a world of luxury brands, eclectic boutiques, and trendy fashion outlets, creating a shopping haven for enthusiasts seeking the latest trends.

2. The Oasis Shopping Centre - Broadbeach: Discover a blend of shopping and alfresco dining at The Oasis Shopping Centre in Broadbeach. Stroll along tree-lined boulevards, explore fashion boutiques, and pause for a delightful meal in this charming shopping precinct.

3. Chevron Renaissance Shopping Centre: Uncover a shopping paradise in the heart of Surfers Paradise at

Chevron Renaissance. With a mix of retail outlets, dining options, and entertainment, this vibrant precinct captures the lively essence of the iconic coastal city.

4. The Village Markets: Embrace the bohemian charm of The Village Markets, held regularly in Burleigh Heads. Browse through stalls featuring fashion, art, and handcrafted treasures while enjoying live music and the laid-back atmosphere of this popular market.

5. Carrara Markets: Delve into one of the largest permanent markets in Australia at Carrara Markets. With over 400 stalls, this market offers everything from arts and crafts to fresh produce, creating a vibrant and diverse shopping experience.

6. Harbour Town Outlet Shopping Centre: Unleash your bargain-hunting spirit at Harbour Town Outlet Shopping Centre. Discover discounted designer brands and outlet stores, making it the perfect destination for those seeking quality at a fraction of the price.

Navigate the Gold Coast's retail landscape, whether you're in search of high-end fashion, unique artisanal creations, or a relaxed market atmosphere. Get ready to indulge in retail revelry as you explore the diverse shopping districts and markets that contribute to the vibrant tapestry of the Gold Coast.

Q1 Skypoint

CHAPTER SIX

Culinary Delights

Culinary Chronicles - Indulging in Gold Coast's Local Cuisine Highlights

Flavors of the Coast:

Embark on a gastronomic journey through the Gold Coast's diverse culinary scene, where fresh seafood, innovative dishes, and local flavors converge to create a dining experience like no other. This chapter unveils the local cuisine highlights that capture the essence of the coastal paradise.

1. Seafood Extravaganza: Savor the ocean's bounty with a seafood feast. From freshly shucked oysters to succulent prawns, indulge in the region's renowned seafood offerings at waterfront restaurants and local eateries.

2. Beachside Cafés in Burleigh Heads: Experience the laid-back charm of Burleigh Heads through its beachside cafés. Enjoy artisanal coffee, freshly baked pastries, and wholesome brunches with the sound of crashing waves as your backdrop.

3. Surfers Paradise Dining Precinct: Immerse yourself in the vibrant dining precinct of Surfers Paradise. Explore a myriad of international cuisines, from Asian fusion to Mediterranean delights, as you dine against the backdrop of the iconic Surfers Paradise skyline.

4. Hinterland Vineyard Experiences: Escape to the lush hinterlands for a vineyard experience. Sample local wines, indulge in gourmet picnics, and soak in the scenic beauty of the Gold Coast's hinterland wineries.

5. Authentic Australian Bush Tucker: Explore the roots of Australian cuisine with bush tucker experiences. From native herbs and spices to dishes incorporating Indigenous ingredients, this culinary adventure offers a taste of Australia's rich food heritage.

6. Food Markets and Food Truck Delights: Discover the diverse and dynamic food markets scattered across the Gold Coast. From NightQuarter to Miami Marketta, indulge in street food delights and global flavors served from food trucks and market stalls.

Savor the distinctive flavors of the Gold Coast, where each bite tells a story of the region's rich culinary heritage. Whether you're indulging in fresh seafood by the ocean or exploring innovative dishes in the city, the local cuisine highlights promise a delightful and mouthwatering journey through the diverse tastes of the coastal paradise. Get ready to embark on a culinary adventure that will tantalize your taste buds and leave you with a lasting appreciation for the Gold Coast's gastronomic offerings.

Culinary Gems - Recommended Restaurants and Cafés

Feast at the Finest:

Indulge your taste buds in the Gold Coast's culinary delights with this curated list of recommended restaurants and cafés. From waterfront fine dining to cozy corner coffee shops, each establishment promises a memorable dining experience.

1. Rick Shores (Burleigh Heads):

- **Location**: 43 Goodwin Tce Shop 3, Gold Coast, Queensland 4220 Australia
- **Phone**: +61 7 5630 6611
- **Price Range**: $19 - $55

- **Special Diets**: Vegetarian Friendly, Vegan Options, Gluten Free Options
- **Meals**: Lunch, Dinner, Late Night, Drinks
- **Cuisines:** Seafood, Asian
- **Features:** Booking, Outdoor Seating, Seating, Parking Available, Street Parking, Highchairs Available, Wheelchair Accessible, Serves Alcohol, Full Bar, Accepts American Express, Accepts Mastercard, Accepts Visa, Accepts Credit Cards, Table Service, Waterfront

Savor Asian-inspired dishes with a beachfront view at Rick Shores. This award-winning restaurant in Burleigh Heads offers a fusion of flavors, with dishes crafted to perfection and a setting that captures the essence of the coastal lifestyle.

2. Baba Joon Persian Grill:

- **Location**: 3106 Surfers Paradise Bvd, Surfers Paradise, Gold Coast, Queensland 4217 Australia
- **Phone**: +61 7 5649 8640
- **Price Range**: $16 - $21
- **Special Diets:** Vegetarian Friendly, Vegan Options
- **Meals:** Dinner, Brunch, Lunch

- **Cuisines:** Mediterranean, Turkish, Grill, Middle Eastern, Persian, Healthy
- **Features:** Booking, Seating, Accepts Credit Cards, Table Service, Delivery, Takeout, Street Parking, Wheelchair Accessible, BYOB, Dog Friendly, Gift Cards Available

3. BSKT Café (Nobby Beach):

- **Location**: 4 Lavarack Rd, Mermaid Beach, Gold Coast, Queensland 4218 Australia
- **Phone**: +61 7 5526 6565
- **Price Range**: NA
- **Special Diets:** Vegetarian Friendly, Vegan Options, Gluten Free Options
- **Meals:** Breakfast, Lunch, Brunch, Drinks
- **Cuisines:** Cafe, Healthy, Australian
- **Features:** Takeout, Outdoor Seating, Seating, Parking Available, Highchairs Available, Wheelchair Accessible, Serves Alcohol, Free Wifi, Accepts Credit Cards, Table Service, Free off-street parking, Wine and Beer, Accepts Mastercard, Accepts Visa, Waterfront, Beach, Playgrounds, Dog Friendly, Family style.

Experience beachside bliss at BSKT Café in Nobby Beach. Known for its health-conscious menu and vibrant atmosphere, this café offers a range of delicious options from nourishing breakfasts to refreshing smoothie bowls.

4. Skypoint Bistro & Bar (Q1 Skypoint) (Surfers Paradise):

- **Location**: 3003 Surfers Paradise Blvd, Surfers Paradise QLD 4217, Australia (on the 77th floor of the Q1 building)
- **Phone**: +61 7 5526 6565
- **Price Range**: Adults: $44.00 and Children (3-13 years): $30.00

Dine amidst the clouds at Skypoint Bistro & Bar. Located atop the Q1 building in Surfers Paradise, this restaurant offers unparalleled views of the coastline, complemented by a diverse menu featuring modern Australian cuisine.

5. The Little Mermaid (Mermaid Beach):

- **Location**: Corner of Sunbrite Ave 1/2557 Gold Coast Highway, Mermaid Beach
- **Phone**: +61 7 5679 8355

Discover the charm of The Little Mermaid, a cozy café in Mermaid Beach. Known for its laid-back atmosphere and delicious menu, it's an ideal spot for a leisurely brunch or afternoon coffee.

6. The Collective Palm Beach (Palm Beach):

- **Location**: 1128 Gold Coast Hwy, Palm Beach, Gold Coast, Queensland 4221 Australia
- **Phone**: +61 7 5618 8229
- **Price Range**: NA
- **Special Diets:** Vegetarian Friendly, Vegan Options, Gluten Free Options
- **Meals:** Lunch, Dinner, Drinks
- **Cuisines:** Italian, Mexican, American, Asian
- **Features:** Highchairs Available, Delivery, Takeout, Booking, Outdoor Seating, Seating, Wheelchair Accessible, Serves Alcohol, Full Bar, Accepts Mastercard, Accepts Visa, Accepts Credit Cards, Table Service, Street Parking, Wine and Beer, Live Music, Non-smoking restaurants, Gift Cards Available

Explore diverse flavors at The Collective Palm Beach, a unique dining destination featuring five kitchens under one roof. From wood-fired pizzas to Asian-inspired dishes, this venue offers a communal dining experience with a vibrant atmosphere.

This section guides you to culinary hotspots that encapsulate the Gold Coast's diverse dining scene. Whether you're seeking fine dining with ocean views or a relaxed café experience, these recommended establishments promise a gastronomic journey that mirrors the coastal paradise's rich and varied flavors. Get ready to embark on a culinary adventure that will leave your taste buds tingling with delight.

CHAPTER SEVEN

Nightlife and Entertainment

Nightlife Revelry - Bars, Clubs, and Entertainment Venues

Cheers to the Night:

Discover the vibrant nightlife of the Gold Coast with this curated guide to bars, clubs, and entertainment venues. From trendy cocktail bars to pulsating dance floors, each venue promises an electrifying experience as you embrace the energetic spirit of the coastal nights.

1. Elsewhere (Surfers Paradise): Dance the night away at Elsewhere, a renowned nightclub in Surfers Paradise. With top-notch DJs, a stylish atmosphere, and a diverse range of music genres, Elsewhere guarantees a memorable and energetic night out.

2. The Island Rooftop (Surfers Paradise): Sip on cocktails with panoramic views at The Island Rooftop. This chic rooftop bar in Surfers Paradise offers a sophisticated setting, live music, and an extensive drinks menu to elevate your nightlife experience.

3. Miami Marketta (Miami): Embrace the eclectic vibe of Miami Marketta, a lively venue that combines a street food market with live music and entertainment. Explore diverse food stalls, sip on craft beers, and dance under the stars in this unique setting.

4. NightQuarter (Helensvale): Experience the vibrant atmosphere of NightQuarter, a night market with a lively entertainment lineup. From live music to street performances, this venue in Helensvale transforms into a cultural hub come nightfall.

5. Stingray Lounge (Surfers Paradise): Unwind in style at Stingray Lounge, a chic cocktail bar in Surfers Paradise. With expert mixologists crafting signature drinks and a stylish ambiance, Stingray Lounge offers a sophisticated retreat for those seeking a laid-back evening.

6. The Avenue (Surfers Paradise): Immerse yourself in the lively atmosphere of The Avenue, a popular venue with a pub-style setting, live music, and a dance floor. Whether you're looking for a casual drink or a night of revelry, The Avenue has you covered.

This section is your ticket to the Gold Coast's after-dark scene, where each venue promises a unique and unforgettable nightlife experience. Whether you're seeking a pulsating dance floor or a relaxed bar with scenic views, these bars, clubs, and entertainment venues invite you to raise a toast to the vibrant coastal nights. Get ready to dive into the electrifying energy of the Gold Coast's nightlife revelry.

Festival Frenzy - Gold Coast's Events and Festivals

Celebrations Beyond the Shore:

Immerse yourself in the festive spirit of the Gold Coast with this guide to the region's lively events and festivals. From cultural celebrations to music extravaganzas, each occasion promises a dynamic and memorable experience that reflects the diverse and vibrant community.

1. Bleach Festival: Celebrate art and culture at the *Bleach Festival*, an annual event that transforms the Gold Coast into a canvas of creativity. From contemporary art installations to live performances, *Bleach Festival* usually takes place in **August, for 2024 (3rd - 13th August 2024)** and showcases the region's artistic prowess.

2. Gold Coast Film Festival: Embrace the magic of the big screen at the Gold Coast Film Festival. Explore a diverse selection of films, attend industry events, and experience the excitement of film premieres, making it a must-attend for cinephiles. The event takes place in the month of **April**.

3. Blues on Broadbeach Music Festival: Feel the rhythm at the Blues on Broadbeach Music Festival. This free event takes over the streets of Broadbeach, featuring an impressive lineup of local and international blues artists. Enjoy live music, food, and a vibrant atmosphere. **The event usually takes place in the month of May. For 2024 (16th - 19th May 2024)**

4. Surfers Paradise Live: Rock to the beats of Surfers Paradise Live, a music festival that transforms the iconic precinct into a stage for live performances. With a focus on Australian artists, this festival brings the streets to life with music, energy, and excitement. **The event usually takes place in the month of May. For 2024 (May 2nd - 5th, 2024)**

5. Cooly Rocks On: Step back in time with Cooly Rocks On, a nostalgic celebration of the 50s and 60s. From classic cars to rock 'n' roll music, this festival in Coolangatta brings retro vibes and a sense of community

GOLD COAST

joy. **The event usually takes place in the month of June. For 2024 (5th - 9th June 2024)**

This section invites you to mark your calendar for these vibrant events and festivals, each adding a unique flavor to the Gold Coast's cultural tapestry. Whether you're a music enthusiast, an art lover, or a sports fan, these celebrations offer an opportunity to connect with the community and experience the dynamic spirit of the coastal paradise. Get ready to join the festival frenzy and create lasting memories amidst the lively atmosphere of the Gold Coast's events calendar.

CHAPTER EIGHT

Family-Friendly Fun

Family Fun - Kid-Friendly Attractions on the Gold Coast

Adventures for All Ages:

Explore a world of family-friendly fun with this guide to kid-approved attractions on the Gold Coast. From thrilling theme parks to interactive wildlife encounters, each destination promises to captivate the imagination of young adventurers.

1. Warner Bros. Movie World: Step into the magic of Warner Bros. Movie World, where beloved characters come to life. From heart-pounding rides to live entertainment featuring superheroes and cartoon favorites, this theme park offers a cinematic adventure for the whole family.

2. Sea World: Dive into the wonders of the ocean at Sea World, a marine-themed park that combines thrilling rides with captivating animal encounters. Watch dolphins, seals, and penguins in action or embark on water-themed adventures designed for family fun.

3. Currumbin Wildlife Sanctuary: Introduce your little ones to Australia's unique wildlife at Currumbin Wildlife Sanctuary. From cuddling koalas to feeding kangaroos, this sanctuary provides an immersive and educational experience in a natural setting.

4. Wet'n'Wild: Make a splash at Wet'n'Wild, the ultimate water park destination on the Gold Coast. With a variety of water slides, wave pools, and family-friendly attractions, it's a haven for water enthusiasts of all ages.

5. Paradise Country: Experience Aussie farm life at Paradise Country, where kids can interact with farm animals, watch live shows, and partake in traditional activities like sheep shearing and boomerang throwing.

6. TreeTop Challenge at Currumbin Wildlife Sanctuary: Elevate the excitement with the TreeTop Challenge, an adventure course nestled in the treetops. Offering a range of challenges suitable for various ages, it's a thrilling way for the whole family to embrace the outdoors.

Whether it's the magic of Movie World, the aquatic wonders of Sea World, or the interactive experiences at Currumbin Wildlife Sanctuary, the Gold Coast promises an array of kid-friendly attractions that create lasting family memories. Get ready to witness the excitement and laughter as you delve into the family-friendly charm of the coastal paradise.

Bonding Beyond the Beach - Family-Oriented Activities on the Gold Coast

Creating Memories Together:

Discover a wealth of family-oriented activities on the Gold Coast that go beyond the sand and surf. From nature adventures to interactive experiences, this chapter provides a guide to activities that will strengthen family bonds and create cherished memories.

1. Hiking in Hinterland National Parks: Embark on family-friendly hikes in the hinterland national parks. Trails like the Purling Brook Falls Circuit offer scenic walks suitable for all ages, providing an opportunity to connect with nature and enjoy breathtaking landscapes.

2. Broadwater Parklands: Unwind at Broadwater Parklands, a waterfront playground offering lush green spaces, playgrounds, and picnic areas. With scenic views of the Broadwater, it's an ideal spot for family picnics, bike rides, and water-based activities.

3. Glow Worm Cave Tour - Springbrook National Park: Embark on a magical journey with a Glow Worm Cave Tour in Springbrook National Park. Witness the enchanting glow of these tiny creatures in a subterranean world, creating a mesmerizing experience for both kids and adults.

4. INFINITY Attraction: Step into the futuristic world of INFINITY, an immersive and mind-bending attraction in Surfers Paradise. This multi-sensory experience offers a unique adventure for families, navigating through dazzling special effects and optical illusions.

5. Putt Putt Golf Mermaid Beach: Enjoy a round of family-friendly fun at Putt Putt Golf in Mermaid Beach. With three unique mini-golf courses, this venue provides a lighthearted and entertaining outing suitable for all skill levels.

6. Gold Coast Aquatic Centre: Dive into aquatic adventures at the Gold Coast Aquatic Centre. With multiple pools, water slides, and family-friendly facilities, it's a perfect destination for a day of swimming and water play.

This section invites families to explore a diverse range of activities that cater to all ages and interests. Whether you're hiking in the hinterland, marveling at glow worms, or enjoying a day of mini-golf, these family-oriented activities promise moments of joy and connection on the Gold Coast. Get ready to create lasting memories as you bond beyond the beach with your loved ones in this coastal paradise.

CHAPTER NINE

Adventure Seekers

Adrenaline Unleashed - Extreme Sports and Adrenaline Activities

Thrill-Seeker's Playground:

For those craving an adrenaline rush, the Gold Coast offers a playground of extreme sports and activities. From soaring heights to racing waves, this chapter guides you through the heart-pounding experiences that will satisfy your appetite for adventure.

1. Skydiving Over the Gold Coast: Elevate your senses with a tandem skydive over the Gold Coast. Experience the rush of free-fall before enjoying a scenic parachute descent with breathtaking views of the coastline.

2. Jetpack Adventures: Defy gravity with Jetpack Adventures, a thrilling water-powered jetpack experience. Soar above the water as you control your flight, making it an exhilarating adventure for adrenaline enthusiasts.

3. V8 Supercar Experience: Rev up your engines with a V8 Supercar driving experience. Feel the power of these high-performance vehicles as you take control on the race track, fulfilling every racing enthusiast's dream.

4. Kitesurfing on Main Beach: Harness the wind and waves with kitesurfing on Main Beach. Whether you're a seasoned kitesurfer or a beginner, the Gold Coast's windy conditions and long stretches of sandy beaches provide an ideal setting for this thrilling water sport.

5. Bungy Jumping at Adrenaline Park: Take the leap with bungy jumping at Adrenaline Park. Nestled in the Gold Coast hinterland, this adrenaline-pumping experience offers a combination of free-fall and rebound, delivering an unforgettable adventure.

6. Off-Road Buggy Adventure: Embark on an off-road buggy adventure through the hinterland. Navigate rugged terrain, splash through mud puddles, and experience the thrill of off-road driving with scenic views as your backdrop.

This section invites thrill-seekers to embrace the extreme side of the Gold Coast. Whether you're free-falling from the sky, mastering a jetpack, or conquering the waves with kitesurfing, these adrenaline-fueled activities promise an unforgettable journey for those who crave excitement and adventure. Get ready to unleash your inner daredevil in this adrenaline seeker's paradise.

Into the Wild - Outdoor Adventure Recommendations on the Gold Coast

Nature's Playground:

Embark on a thrilling outdoor adventure on the Gold Coast, where diverse landscapes offer a canvas for adrenaline-pumping activities and nature exploration. This chapter serves as your guide to the best outdoor adventures, from soaring heights to exploring hidden gems.

1. Hot Air Ballooning at Sunrise: Rise with the sun and take to the skies with hot air ballooning over the Gold Coast hinterland. Witness breathtaking landscapes as you float above rolling hills, vineyards, and the sparkling coastline.

2. Kayaking in Currumbin Creek: Paddle through the serene waters of Currumbin Creek on a kayaking adventure. Explore mangrove-lined waterways, spot wildlife, and enjoy the tranquility of this hidden gem nestled in the heart of the Gold Coast.

3. Hinterland Horseback Riding: Discover the hinterland on horseback with a scenic trail ride. Traverse through lush rainforests, open meadows, and mountain trails, immersing yourself in the natural beauty of the Gold Coast hinterland.

4. Abseiling in the Springbrook National Park: Challenge yourself with abseiling adventures in Springbrook National Park. Descend down waterfalls and cliffs under the guidance of experienced instructors, combining adrenaline with the thrill of exploring cascading landscapes.

5. Stand-Up Paddleboarding at Tallebudgera Creek: Navigate the calm waters of Tallebudgera Creek with stand-up paddleboarding. Enjoy a leisurely paddle, soak in the picturesque surroundings, and perhaps even spot marine life beneath the crystal-clear waters.

6. Mountain Biking in Nerang National Park: Hit the trails for mountain biking adventures in Nerang National Park. With a network of tracks catering to various skill levels, it's an exhilarating way to explore the rugged beauty of the hinterland.

This section invites outdoor enthusiasts to embrace the Gold Coast's natural wonders through thrilling activities and adventures. Whether you're soaring in a hot air balloon, exploring hidden creeks, or tackling mountain bike trails, the region offers an outdoor playground for those seeking excitement and connection with nature. Get ready to venture into the wild and make memories in the diverse landscapes of the Gold Coast.

CHAPTER TEN

Cultural Immersion

Cultural Odyssey - Museums and Art Galleries on the Gold Coast

Exploring Art and Heritage:

Delve into the cultural tapestry of the Gold Coast with this guide to museums and art galleries. From contemporary art spaces to historical exhibitions, this chapter invites you to immerse yourself in the rich heritage and creative expressions of the coastal paradise.

1. Home of the Arts (HOTA): Embark on a cultural journey at Home of the Arts (HOTA). This dynamic cultural precinct in Surfers Paradise features an art gallery, outdoor stages, and a cinema, providing a platform for diverse artistic experiences, exhibitions, and performances.

2. Gold Coast City Gallery: Explore contemporary art at the Gold Coast City Gallery, located within The Arts Centre Gold Coast. With a focus on contemporary and modern Australian art, the gallery hosts exhibitions, workshops, and events throughout the year.

3. Wax Museum: Step into the world of wax figures at the Wax Museum in Surfers Paradise. This unique attraction features lifelike wax sculptures of celebrities, historical figures, and cultural icons, offering an entertaining and educational experience for visitors of all ages.

4. Australian Outback Spectacular: Celebrate Australia's heritage at the Australian Outback Spectacular. Combining live performances, horsemanship, and special effects, this unique dinner show provides a theatrical journey into the heart of the Australian outback.

5. Surf World Gold Coast: Dive into the history of surfing at Surf World Gold Coast in Currumbin. This museum showcases the evolution of surfing culture, featuring vintage surfboards, memorabilia, and interactive exhibits that capture the essence of the region's coastal lifestyle.

6. The Walls Art Space: Experience contemporary art at The Walls Art Space in Miami. This artist-run initiative provides a platform for emerging and experimental art practices, offering a dynamic space for exhibitions, performances, and artistic collaborations.

This section invites cultural enthusiasts to explore the diverse cultural offerings of the Gold Coast. Whether you're admiring contemporary art at HOTA, delving into the world of wax sculptures, or immersing yourself in the history of surfing, the museums and art galleries of the Gold Coast promise a cultural odyssey that enriches the mind and captivates the soul. Get ready to unravel the artistic and historical threads woven into the fabric of this vibrant coastal community.

Cultural Revelry - Gold Coast's Cultural Events and Festivals

Celebrating Diversity and Creativity:

Immerse yourself in the cultural vibrancy of the Gold Coast with this guide to the region's diverse cultural events and festivals. From multicultural celebrations to artistic showcases, this chapter invites you to partake in the rich tapestry of cultural revelry.

1. Bleach Festival: Celebrate creativity and culture at *Bleach Festival*, an annual event that transforms the Gold Coast into a dynamic arts and cultural hub. It takes place over 11 days in **August**, featuring a mix of contemporary art installations, live performances, and community events, *Bleach Festival* is a highlight for culture enthusiasts.

2. Gold Coast Multicultural Festival: Embrace diversity at the Gold Coast Multicultural Festival. This annual one-day event, typically held in **September**, showcases the rich tapestry of cultures that call the Gold Coast home, featuring music, dance, food, and traditions from around the world.

3. SWELL Sculpture Festival: Experience art in the open air at the SWELL Sculpture Festival. Held annually in the **second week of September** along the stunning Currumbin Beach, this outdoor exhibition features captivating sculptures created by local and international artists, offering a unique blend of creativity and coastal beauty.

4. Gold Coast Film Festival: Indulge in the cinematic arts at the Gold Coast Film Festival. Showcasing a diverse selection of films, from international features to locally produced gems, this festival provides a platform for filmmakers and film enthusiasts to come together. The festival's main venue is the Home of the Arts (HOTA) in Surfers Paradise, but events are also held at other locations across the Gold Coast.

5. Surfers Paradise Festival: Join the festivities at the Surfers Paradise Festival, an annual celebration that brings the iconic precinct to life. With a lineup of live music, art exhibitions, and street performances, this event captures the lively spirit of Surfers Paradise.

6. Gold Coast Open House: Unlock the doors to the city's architectural gems during the Gold Coast Open House. This annual event, takes place in **October**, offers the public a rare opportunity to explore a variety of significant buildings, showcasing the city's evolving architectural landscape.

This section invites you to immerse yourself in the cultural heartbeat of the Gold Coast through a calendar of events that celebrate diversity, creativity, and community spirit. Whether you're strolling through a sculpture festival on the beach or enjoying the festivities of a multicultural event, these cultural celebrations promise an enriching and vibrant experience. Get ready to join the cultural revelry and connect with the heart and soul of the Gold Coast.

CHAPTER ELEVEN

Gold Coast Tours

Conquering the Gold Coast: A Tour Guide for Every Traveler

The Gold Coast shimmers with sun-kissed beaches, dazzling theme parks, and a hinterland teeming with lush rainforests. But beyond the iconic sights, adventure awaits around every corner. To delve deeper, dive into the world of captivating tours, designed to ignite your passions and leave you with memories etched in gold.

Nature's Embrace: Rainforest Delights

Gold Coast Hinterland Tour with Adventure Tours Australia:

Embrace the emerald embrace of the hinterland. Kayak on pristine waterways, marvel at cascading waterfalls like Purlingbrook Falls, and spot elusive native wildlife (Koala cuddles anyone?).

- **Duration**: 6 hours
- **Price**: ~$149
- **Contact**: https://www.adventuretours.com.au/

Springbrook & Tamborine National Park Glow Worm Tour with EcoQuest:

Hike through ancient rainforests, witness the breathtaking Natural Bridge, and descend into a hidden cavern where thousands of tiny glowworms illuminate the night sky.

- **Duration**: 4 hours
- **Price**: ~$99
- **Contact**: https://www.getyourguide.com/brisbane-l300/from-brisbane-rainforest-and-glow-worm-tour-t68262/

Thrills & Spills: Adrenaline Adventures
Jet Boating with Jet Boat Extreme:

Buckle up for an exhilarating ride on the Broadwater, weaving through stunning scenery and experiencing heart-pounding 360° spins.

- **Duration**: 30 minutes
- **Price**: ~$89
- **Contact**: https://www.jetboatextreme.com.au/

Parasailing with Gold Coast Parasail:

Soar above the iconic Surfers Paradise skyline, feeling the wind in your hair and the vast Pacific Ocean stretching beneath you.

- **Duration**: 10-15 minutes
- **Price**: ~$79
- **Contact**: https://www.goldcoastwatersports.com/parasailing/

Wildlife Encounters: Unforgettable Connections

Currumbin Wildlife Sanctuary Tour:

Encounter Australia's iconic animals – cuddly koalas, majestic cassowaries, playful otters – and witness spectacular bird shows and feeding demonstrations.

- **Duration**: Full day
- **Price**: ~$69
- **Contact**: https://currumbinsanctuary.com.au/

Dolphin Kayaking Tour with Ocean Kayak Adventures:

Paddle across the calm waters of Moreton Island, searching for playful pods of dolphins and enjoying breathtaking island views. Duration: 4 hours, Price: ~$135. Contact: https://www.australiankayakingadventures.com.au/

Cultural Immersion: Local Gems

Gold Coast Food & Wine Tour with Epicurean Food Tours:

Embark on a culinary adventure, savoring the region's finest gourmet delights from award-winning restaurants, boutique producers, and hidden gems.

- **Duration**: 4 hours
- **Price**: ~$180
- **Contact**: https://www.epicureantours.com.au/

Surfers Paradise History Walk with Tales of the Gold Coast:

Uncover the stories behind the glitz and glamour, exploring iconic landmarks and learning about the city's fascinating transformation.

- **Duration**: 2 hours

- Price: ~$49

- Contact: https://www.goldcoast.qld.gov.au/Things-to-do/Gold-Coast-Events-Calendar/Eventbrite/NaturallyGC-Nocturnal-Natives-656451432907

Remember:

- This is just a starting point - research further to find tours that perfectly match your interests and budget.

- Consider smaller, eco-friendly tour operators for a more personalized and sustainable experience.

- Book tours in advance, especially during peak season, to secure your spot.

- Comfortable shoes, sunscreen, and a sense of adventure are your essential travel companions!

-

CHAPTER TWELVE

Accommodation Guide

Stay and Play - Overview of Different Areas to Stay on the Gold Coast

Finding Your Coastal Haven:

Explore the diverse neighborhoods and coastal havens that make up the Gold Coast. This chapter serves as your guide to different areas to stay, each offering a unique blend of scenery, amenities, and atmosphere. Whether you seek beachfront luxury or hinterland tranquility, discover the perfect base for your Gold Coast adventure.

1. Surfers Paradise: The iconic heart of the Gold Coast, Surfers Paradise, is known for its vibrant atmosphere, high-rise skyline, and world-renowned surf beaches. Offering a mix of accommodation, dining, and entertainment options, it's a bustling hub for those seeking an energetic coastal experience.

2. Broadbeach: A sophisticated coastal enclave, Broadbeach boasts a thriving dining and shopping scene. With its pristine beaches, upscale resorts, and proximity to Pacific Fair Shopping Centre, it's an ideal choice for those desiring a blend of luxury and leisure.

3. Burleigh Heads: Embrace a laid-back beachside vibe in Burleigh Heads. This area is renowned for its surfing culture, the scenic Burleigh Head National Park, and a range of eclectic boutiques and cafés. It's a perfect choice for those seeking a relaxed coastal lifestyle.

4. Southport: Nestled along the Broadwater, Southport offers a more tranquil setting with parks, marinas, and family-friendly attractions. It's a central location, providing easy access to both the beaches and the vibrant culture of the city.

5. Mermaid Beach: Experience the charm of Mermaid Beach, a quieter residential area with a mix of holiday rentals and boutique accommodations. It's an excellent choice for those wanting a more secluded stay while remaining close to the coastal action.

6. Hinterland Retreats: Escape to the lush hinterland for a tranquil retreat. Areas like Tamborine Mountain and Springbrook offer secluded cabins, bed and breakfasts, and stunning views of the hinterland landscapes. Perfect for those seeking a peaceful and nature-centric escape.

This section guides you through the diverse neighborhoods, each offering its own flavor of the Gold Coast experience. Whether you prefer the lively energy of Surfers Paradise, the sophistication of Broadbeach, or the tranquility of the hinterland, you'll find the perfect setting for your stay on the Gold Coast. Get ready to find your coastal haven and make the most of your time in this dynamic and beautiful destination.

Coastal Comforts - Recommendations for Various Budgets on the Gold Coast

Finding Your Perfect Retreat:

Discover accommodations tailored to different budgets on the Gold Coast, ensuring that every traveler can experience the beauty of this coastal paradise. From budget-friendly stays to luxurious escapes, this chapter provides recommendations to suit various financial preferences.

1. Budget-Friendly Retreats:

Surfers Paradise:

HI Surfers Paradise Beachfront Hostel:

- **Price**: $25-35 per night.

- **Description**: This lively hostel features dorms and private rooms, a rooftop pool, and stunning ocean views. It's perfect for social travelers and backpackers.
- **Nearby attractions**: Surfers Paradise Beach, SkyPoint Observation Deck, Infinity Attraction.

Chevron Renaissance Apartments:

- **Price**: $50-70 per night.
- **Description**: This apartment complex offers affordable self-contained apartments with kitchen facilities. It's a good option for families or groups who want more space and privacy.
- **Nearby attractions**: Q1 Building, Cavill Avenue shopping precinct, Kurrawa Beach.

Gold Coast International Hotel:

- **Price**: $60-80 per night.
- **Description**: This hotel offers basic budget-friendly rooms with comfortable amenities. It's centrally located and walking distance to many attractions.

- **Nearby attractions**: Surfers Paradise Beach, Ripley's Believe It or Not! Odditorium, Infinity Attraction.

Broadbeach:

Meriton Broadbeach on the Beach:

- **Price**: $70-90 per night.
- **Description**: This apartment complex offers affordable studio and one-bedroom apartments with stunning ocean views. It has a great location on the beachfront and close to shops and restaurants.
- **Nearby attractions**: Kurrawa Beach, The Star Gold Coast casino, Pacific Fair Shopping Centre.

Beach Haven Resort Broadbeach:

- **Price**: $80-100 per night.
- **Description**: This resort offers spacious one and two-bedroom apartments with kitchen facilities and a swimming pool. It's a family-friendly option with a relaxed atmosphere.
- **Nearby attractions**: Kurrawa Beach, The Spit Gold Coast, Pacific Fair Shopping Centre.

Watermark Resort Broadbeach:

- **Price**: $90-110 per night.
- **Description**: This resort offers one and two-bedroom apartments with balconies and some ocean views. It has a swimming pool and spa, and is located close to shops and restaurants.
- **Nearby attractions**: Kurrawa Beach, The Star Gold Coast casino, Pacific Fair Shopping Centre.

Coolangatta:

Coolangatta Backpackers Hostel:

- **Price**: $20-30 per night.
- **Description**: This hostel offers dorms and private rooms, a swimming pool, and a relaxed atmosphere. It's perfect for budget-conscious travelers and surfers.
- **Nearby attractions**: Coolangatta Beach, Kirra Beach, Snapper Rocks surf break.

Oaks Gold Coast Hotel:

- **Price**: $55-75 per night.

- **Description**: This hotel offers modern rooms with balconies and some ocean views. It has a swimming pool and is located close to shops and restaurants.
- **Nearby attractions**: Coolangatta Beach, Kirra Beach, Snapper Rocks surf break.

Reflections Coolangatta Beach Apartments:

- **Price**: $80-100 per night.
- **Description**: This apartment complex offers one and two-bedroom apartments with stunning ocean views. It has a swimming pool, spa, and BBQ facilities.
- **Nearby attractions**: Coolangatta Beach, Kirra Beach, Snapper Rocks surf break.

2. Mid-Range Comfort:

Surfers Paradise:

Mantra Circle on Cavill Apartments:

- **Address**: 3137 Surfers Paradise Blvd, Surfers Paradise QLD 4217, Australia.
- **Price**: $150-200 per night.
- **Description**: Modern 1, 2, and 3 bedroom apartments with balconies, some with ocean views.

Facilities include a swimming pool, spa, sauna, and gym. Great location on Cavill Avenue, close to shops, restaurants, and nightlife.
- **Nearby attractions**: Surfers Paradise Beach, SkyPoint Observation Deck, Infinity Attraction.

Meriton Suites Broadbeach:

- **Address**: 1320 Gold Coast Hwy, Broadbeach QLD 4218, Australia.
- **Price**: $120-180 per night.
- **Description**: Spacious studio, 1, 2, and 3 bedroom apartments with balconies, some with ocean views. Facilities include a swimming pool, spa, sauna, and gym. Located opposite the beach and close to restaurants and shops.
- **Nearby attractions**: Kurrawa Beach, The Star Gold Coast casino, Pacific Fair Shopping Centre.

QT Gold Coast:

- **Address**: 7 Staunton St, Surfers Paradise QLD 4217, Australia.
- **Price**: $200-250 per night.
- **Description**: Stylish boutique hotel with rooftop bar and stunning ocean views. Rooms are modern

and well-appointed, with some featuring balconies and spa baths. Close to beaches, nightlife, and attractions.

- **Nearby attractions**: Surfers Paradise Beach, SkyPoint Observation Deck, Infinity Attraction.

Coolangatta:

Oaks Oasis Resort:

- **Address**: 272-294 Griffith St, Coolangatta QLD 4211, Australia.
- **Price**: $130-170 per night.
- **Description**: Resort-style apartments with 1, 2, and 3 bedroom options, all with balconies and some with ocean views. Facilities include a swimming pool, spa, sauna, gym, and BBQ area. Close to the beach, airport, and Coolangatta restaurants and shops.
- **Nearby attractions**: Coolangatta Beach, Kirra Beach, Snapper Rocks surf break.

GOLD COAST

The Strand Coolangatta Beach:

- **Address**: 358 David Low Way, Coolangatta QLD 4211, Australia.
- **Price**: $180-230 per night.
- **Description**: Modern hotel with stylish rooms and balconies, some with ocean views. Facilities include a rooftop bar and restaurant, swimming pool, and gym. Located directly on the beach and close to Coolangatta shops and restaurants.
- **Nearby attractions**: Coolangatta Beach, Kirra Beach, Snapper Rocks surf break.

Halcyon Pacific Resort:

- **Address**: 76-80 Pacific Blvd, Coolangatta QLD 4211, Australia.
- **Price**: $190-240 per night. Description: Luxury resort apartments with 1, 2, and 3 bedroom options, all with balconies and stunning ocean views. Facilities include multiple swimming pools, a spa, sauna, gym, and BBQ area. Located directly on the beach and close to Coolangatta restaurants and shops.
- **Nearby attractions**: Coolangatta Beach, Kirra Beach, Snapper Rocks surf break.

3. Luxury Escapes:

Surfers Paradise:

Palazzo Versace:

- **Address**: 97 Seaworld Dr, Main Beach QLD 4217, Australia.
- **Price**: $800-2,000+ per night.
- **Description**: Iconic luxury hotel inspired by an Italian palace, featuring opulent rooms, suites, and villas with private pools. Facilities include multiple restaurants, bars, a day spa, casino, and private beach access.
- **Nearby attractions**: Surfers Paradise Beach, SkyPoint Observation Deck, Infinity Attraction.

The Star Grand at The Star Gold Coast:

- **Address**: 1 Casino Dr, Broadbeach QLD 4218, Australia.
- **Price**: $600-1,500+ per night.
- **Description**: Integrated resort featuring luxurious rooms, suites, and villas. Facilities include multiple restaurants, bars, casino, day spa, nightclubs, and a lagoon pool. Close to beaches, shopping, and dining.

- **Nearby attractions**: Kurrawa Beach, The Star Gold Coast casino, Pacific Fair Shopping Centre.

InterContinental Sanctuary Cove Resort:

- **Address**: 2 Manor Dr, Sanctuary Cove QLD 4212, Australia.
- **Price**: $500-1,200+ per night.
- **Description**: Luxurious waterfront resort nestled within a marina. Spacious rooms, suites, and villas feature balconies or patios with water views. Facilities include multiple restaurants, bars, day spa, pools, gym, and tennis courts.
- **Nearby attractions**: Sanctuary Cove Marina, Gold Coast Hinterland, Mount Tamborine.

Coolangatta:

The Ritz-Carlton, Coolangatta:

- **Address**: 15 Goodwin Tce, Coolangatta QLD 4211, Australia.
- **Price**: $700-1,800+ per night.
- **Description**: Luxurious beachfront hotel with stunning ocean views. Stylish rooms, suites, and residences feature balconies or terraces. Facilities include multiple restaurants, bars, day spa, pool,

and fitness center. Close to beaches, surfing, and dining.

- **Nearby attractions**: Coolangatta Beach, Kirra Beach, Snapper Rocks surf break.

Halcyon House:

- **Address**: 278-282 Pacific Blvd, Coolangatta QLD 4211, Australia.
- **Price**: $400-1,000+ per night.
- **Description**: Boutique luxury hotel with stunning ocean views. Individually designed rooms, suites, and penthouses feature balconies or terraces. Facilities include a restaurant, bar, day spa, pool, and rooftop terrace. Close to beaches, surfing, and dining.
- **Nearby attractions**: Coolangatta Beach, Kirra Beach, Snapper Rocks surf break.

Sofitel Broadbeach:

- **Address**: 3000 Gold Coast Hwy, Broadbeach QLD 4218, Australia.
- **Price**: $450-1,100+ per night.
- **Description**: Luxury beachfront hotel with panoramic ocean views. Stylish rooms, suites, and

apartments feature balconies or terraces. Facilities include multiple restaurants, bars, day spa, pool, and fitness center. Close to beaches, shopping, and dining.

- **Nearby attractions**: Kurrawa Beach, The Star Gold Coast casino, Pacific Fair Shopping Centre.

4. Boutique and Unique:

Surfers Paradise:

Peppers Soul Surfers Paradise:

- **Address**: 30 The Esplanade, Surfers Paradise QLD 4217, Australia.
- **Price**: $250-400+ per night.
- **Description**: This stylish hotel boasts a relaxed, beachy vibe with stunning ocean views. Rooms are modern and feature balconies, some with private plunge pools. Enjoy the rooftop bar, restaurant, and infinity pool, all within walking distance of Surfers Paradise Beach, SkyPoint Observation Deck, and Infinity Attraction.

The Island Gold Coast:

- **Address**: 7060 Gold Coast Hwy, Surfers Paradise QLD 4217, Australia.

- **Price**: $400-600+ per night.
- **Description**: This unique hotel offers streamlined quarters in a contemporary setting. Relax in your stylish room or suite, enjoy the restaurant, bar, and game lounge, or take a dip in the rooftop pool with stunning city views.
- **Nearby attracyions:** Surfers Paradise Beach, SkyPoint Observation Deck, and Infinity Attraction.

Watermark Surfers Paradise:

- **Address**: 3000 Gold Coast Hwy, Broadbeach QLD 4218, Australia.
- **Price**: $350-500+ per night.
- **Description**: This boutique hotel offers a sophisticated escape with panoramic ocean views. Indulge in luxurious rooms or suites with balconies, unwind at the rooftop spa and infinity pool, or savor local cuisine at the restaurant.
- **Nearby attractions**: Surfers Paradise Beach, SkyPoint Observation Deck, and Infinity Attraction.

Coolangatta:

Kirra Surf Apartments:

- **Address**: 149 David Low Way, Coolangatta QLD 4211, Australia.
- **Price**: $200-300+ per night.
- **Description**: Immerse yourself in the surfer lifestyle at these beachfront apartments. Enjoy ocean views from your balcony, take a dip in the pool, or catch some waves just steps away. Kirra Beach, Snapper Rocks surf break, and Coolangatta restaurants and shops are all within walking distance.

Halcyon Pacific Resort:

- **Address**: 76-80 Pacific Blvd, Coolangatta QLD 4211, Australia.
- **Price**: $400-600+ per night.
- **Description**: Experience luxury with a touch of whimsy at this resort. Relax in your spacious apartment with stunning ocean views, unwind at the multiple pools, indulge in treatments at the day spa, or enjoy a meal at one of the restaurants. It's

close to Coolangatta Beach, Kirra Beach, and Snapper Rocks surf break.

QT Coolangatta:

- **Address**: 170 Griffith St, Coolangatta QLD 4211, Australia.
- **Price**: $300-450+ per night.
- **Description**: Embrace bold design and vibrant energy at this quirky hotel. Rooms are playful and feature balconies, some with ocean views. Enjoy the rooftop bar, restaurant, and pool, or explore the nearby Coolangatta Beach, Kirra Beach, and Snapper Rocks surf break.

Tamborine Mountain:

Pethers Rainforest Retreat:

- **Address**: 28b Geissmann St, Tamborine Mountain QLD 4519, Australia.
- **Price**: $300-500+ per night.
- **Description**: Escape to the serenity of the rainforest at this adults-only retreat. Each self-contained cottage is uniquely themed and features a spa bath and fireplace. Relax in the communal

hot tub, explore the surrounding rainforest trails, or visit nearby wineries and waterfalls.

Lisson Grove Boutique Resort & Day Spa:

- **Address**: 274-280 Main Western Rd, Tamborine Mountain QLD 4519, Australia.
- **Price**: $250-400+ per night.
- **Description**: Step back in time at this charming Tudor-style retreat. Choose from individually themed cottages or suites, all featuring spa baths and log fireplaces. Enjoy the day spa, swimming pool, tennis court, and onsite restaurant, or explore the nearby wineries, galleries, and waterfalls.

Gold Coast Hinterland:

Mt Warning Rainforest Cottages:

- **Address**: 305-347 Old Beaudesert Rd, Scenic Rim QLD 4285, Australia.
- **Price**: $200-300+ per night.
- **Description**: Nestled amidst lush rainforest, these cozy cottages offer a tranquil escape. Enjoy fireplaces, spa baths, and private decks with

stunning mountain views. Hike Mount Warning National Park, explore nearby wineries and farms, or simply relax in the serenity of the forest.

Binna Burra Sky Lodges:

- **Address**: Binna Burra Rd, Binna Burra QLD 4211, Australia.
- **Price**: $350-500+ per night.
- **Description**: Experience breathtaking mountain views from these eco-friendly timber lodges perched on the edge of the McPherson Ranges. Relax in your lodge with a balcony and fireplace, explore walking trails, visit the nearby Lamington National Park, or unwind at the onsite restaurant.

The Spa Retreat at Spicers Tamarind:

- **Address**: 8822 Beaudesert Rd, Canungra QLD 4507, Australia.
- **Price**: $400-600+ per night.
- **Description**: Indulge in ultimate relaxation at this luxury spa retreat nestled amidst rainforest foothills. Relax in your luxurious suite with a fireplace and balcony, indulge in spa treatments,

enjoy the onsite restaurants and bars, or explore the surrounding hiking trails and waterfalls.

Southern Gold Coast:

Beachwood Resort:

- **Address**: 83-109 Marine Pde, Cudgen Headland NSW 2484, Australia.
- **Price**: $250-400+ per night.
- **Description**: Embrace coastal living at this beachfront resort surrounded by national parks. Choose from beach bungalows, apartments, or villas, all featuring balconies and some with ocean views. Enjoy the pool, tennis court, playground, and direct access to the beach, or explore the nearby Tweed Coast hinterland and Currumbin Wildlife Sanctuary.

Salt Beach Retreat:

- **Address**: 42 Pacific Dr, Fingal Head NSW 2485, Australia.
- **Price**: $400-600+ per night.
- **Description**: Experience barefoot luxury at this eco-conscious beachfront retreat. Relax in your stylish villa with a plunge pool and ocean views,

indulge in sustainable dining at the onsite restaurant, or explore the nearby beaches, national parks, and cafes of Fingal Head.

Kiff & Culture Palm Beach:

- **Address**: 155 Pacific Parade, Palm Beach QLD 4221, Australia.
- **Price**: $300-450+ per night.
- **Description**: Immerse yourself in coastal chic at this stylish boutique hotel. Relax in your modern room or apartment with a balcony and some ocean views, enjoy the rooftop pool and bar, or explore the nearby cafes, beaches, and boutiques of Palm Beach.

This section ensures that every traveler, regardless of budget, can find the perfect retreat on the Gold Coast. Whether you prefer a budget-friendly hostel in Surfers Paradise, a mid-range apartment in Mermaid Beach, or a luxury escape at Palazzo Versace, there's a coastal haven awaiting you. Get ready to choose the accommodation that aligns with your budget and enhances your Gold Coast experience.

CHAPTER THIRTEEN

Practical Tips

Cultural Courtesies - Local Customs and Etiquette on the Gold Coast

Navigating Social Graces:

Before you embark on your Gold Coast adventure, familiarize yourself with the local customs and etiquette to ensure a respectful and enjoyable experience. This chapter provides insights into the cultural nuances that will help you connect with the community and embrace the coastal lifestyle.

1. Casual Beachwear:

- Embrace the laid-back atmosphere by wearing casual beach attire in coastal areas.

- However, dress appropriately when visiting restaurants, theaters, or upscale venues.

2. Greetings:

- Australians generally use a friendly and informal style of greeting.

- A simple "G'day" or "Hello" is commonly used, accompanied by a smile and direct eye contact.

3. Tipping:

- Tipping is appreciated but not mandatory. In restaurants, leaving around 10% is customary if service is not included.

- Tipping is less common in casual settings or when receiving services like taxis and coffee.

4. Queueing:

- Australians value orderly queues. Wait your turn in lines and maintain a respectful distance from others.

5. Outdoor Culture:

- Embrace outdoor activities and socializing. The Gold Coast's climate encourages a lifestyle that revolves around outdoor spaces, parks, and beaches.

6. Respect for Nature:

- Show respect for the environment. Dispose of rubbish properly and follow conservation guidelines, especially in natural areas.

7. Informal Conversations:

- Australians engage in friendly and informal conversations. Small talk is common, and humor is appreciated.

8. Respect for Indigenous Culture:

- Acknowledge and respect the rich Indigenous culture of Australia. Take the time to learn about the history and significance of the land.

9. Driving Etiquette:

- Follow traffic rules diligently. Australians drive on the left side of the road, and seat belts are mandatory for all passengers.

10. Beach Etiquette:

- Follow beach etiquette by respecting designated swimming areas, observing safety signs, and avoiding loud or disruptive behavior.

By embracing these local customs and etiquette, you'll find yourself seamlessly blending into the Gold Coast's vibrant community. Whether you're enjoying the beach culture, engaging in casual conversations, or showing respect for the environment, these social graces will enhance your experience and make your time on the Gold Coast even more enjoyable.

Safe and Sound - Safety and Health Information on the Gold Coast

Prioritizing Your Well-Being:

Before embarking on your Gold Coast journey, familiarize yourself with essential safety and health information. This chapter provides valuable insights to ensure your well-being, whether you're exploring the beaches, hinterland, or vibrant cityscape.

1. Emergency Services:

- In case of emergencies, dial 000 for immediate assistance (police, fire, ambulance).

- Memorize the local contact numbers for non-emergencies and medical assistance.

2. Sun Safety:

- The Gold Coast enjoys abundant sunshine. Protect yourself from UV rays by using sunscreen, wearing hats, and seeking shade during peak sunlight hours.

- Stay hydrated, especially in warm weather, by drinking plenty of water.

3. Ocean Safety:

- Swim only in designated areas patrolled by lifeguards.

- Obey beach safety signs and flags indicating current conditions.

- If caught in a rip current, float and raise your arm for assistance.

4. Wildlife Caution:

- Admire wildlife from a safe distance. Some species, such as jellyfish and certain spiders, can be harmful.

- If stung by a marine creature, seek immediate medical attention.

5. Healthcare Facilities:

- Familiarize yourself with the locations of hospitals, medical clinics, and pharmacies.

- Carry essential medications and a basic first aid kit.

6. Drinking Water:

- Tap water is safe to drink across the Gold Coast. Refill reusable water bottles to stay hydrated.

7. COVID-19 Guidelines:

- Stay informed about current COVID-19 guidelines and restrictions.

- Adhere to public health measures and practice good hygiene.

8. Public Transport Safety:

- Follow safety guidelines on public transportation.

- Be vigilant with personal belongings in crowded areas.

9. Hiking and Outdoor Safety:

- If engaging in outdoor activities, inform someone of your plans.

- Wear appropriate footwear, carry water, and be aware of your surroundings.

10. Travel Insurance:

- Consider purchasing travel insurance to cover unexpected medical expenses and travel disruptions.

By prioritizing safety and health, you can fully enjoy your Gold Coast experience. Whether you're basking in the sun on the beaches, exploring the hinterland, or navigating the city, these precautions will contribute to a safe and sound journey.

CHAPTER FOURTEEN

Gold Coast Toolkit

Navigating the Coast - Maps and Useful Contacts on the Gold Coast

Your Guide to Resources:

Ensure a seamless journey on the Gold Coast by having access to maps and useful contacts. This chapter provides information on maps to navigate the region and contacts that can assist you during your stay.

1. Maps:

- *Google Maps:* Utilize the convenience of Google Maps for real-time navigation, whether you're exploring the beaches, hinterland, or urban areas.

- *Gold Coast Tourism Map:* Obtain a physical or digital copy of the Gold Coast tourism map from local information centers, highlighting key attractions, accommodations, and points of interest.

GOLD COAST

Map of Surfers Paradise

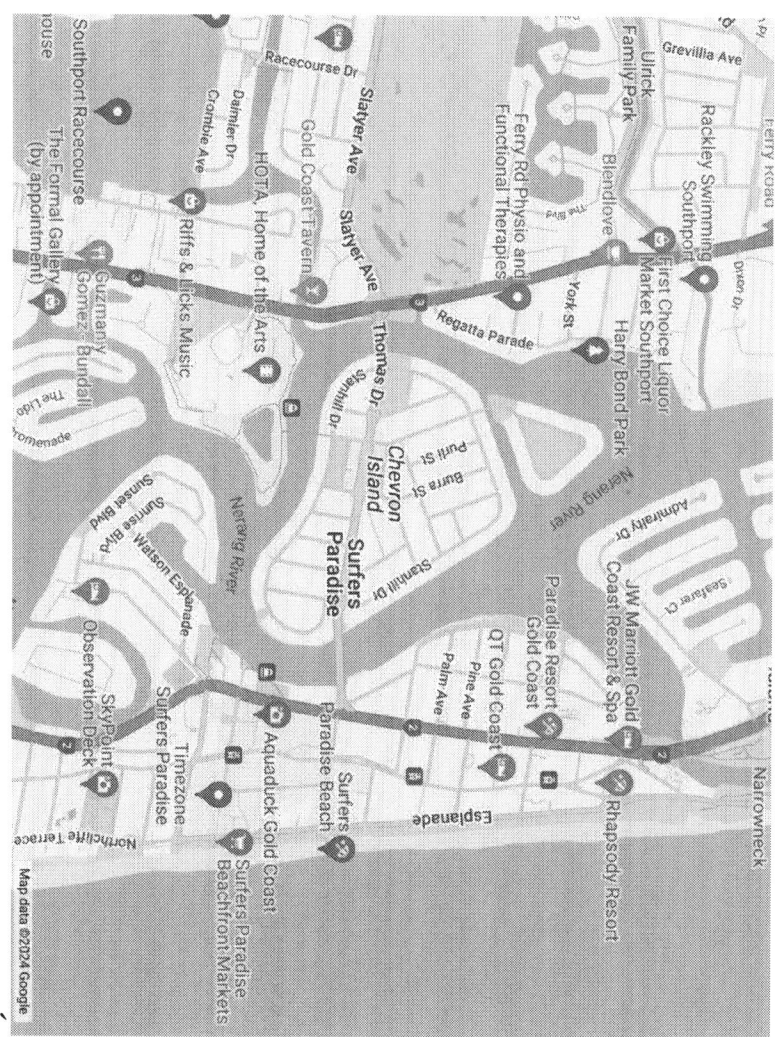

GOLD COAST

Map of Broadbeach

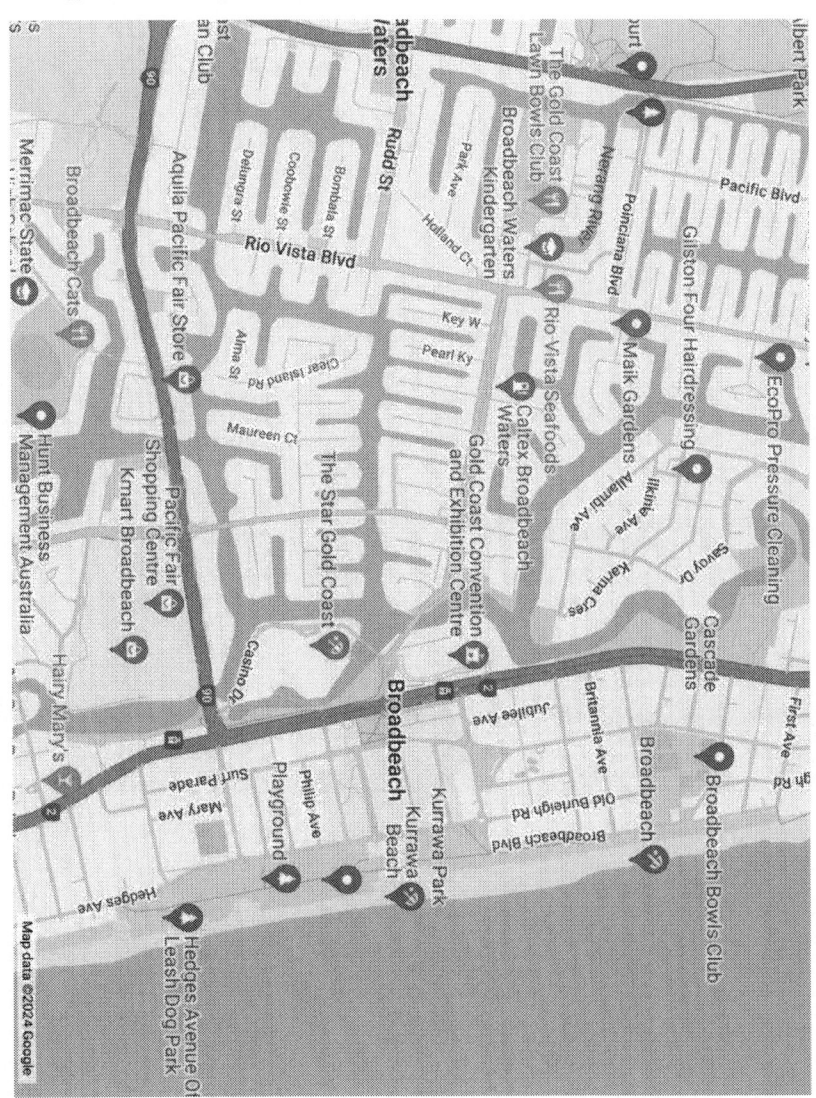

Map of Surfers Paradise

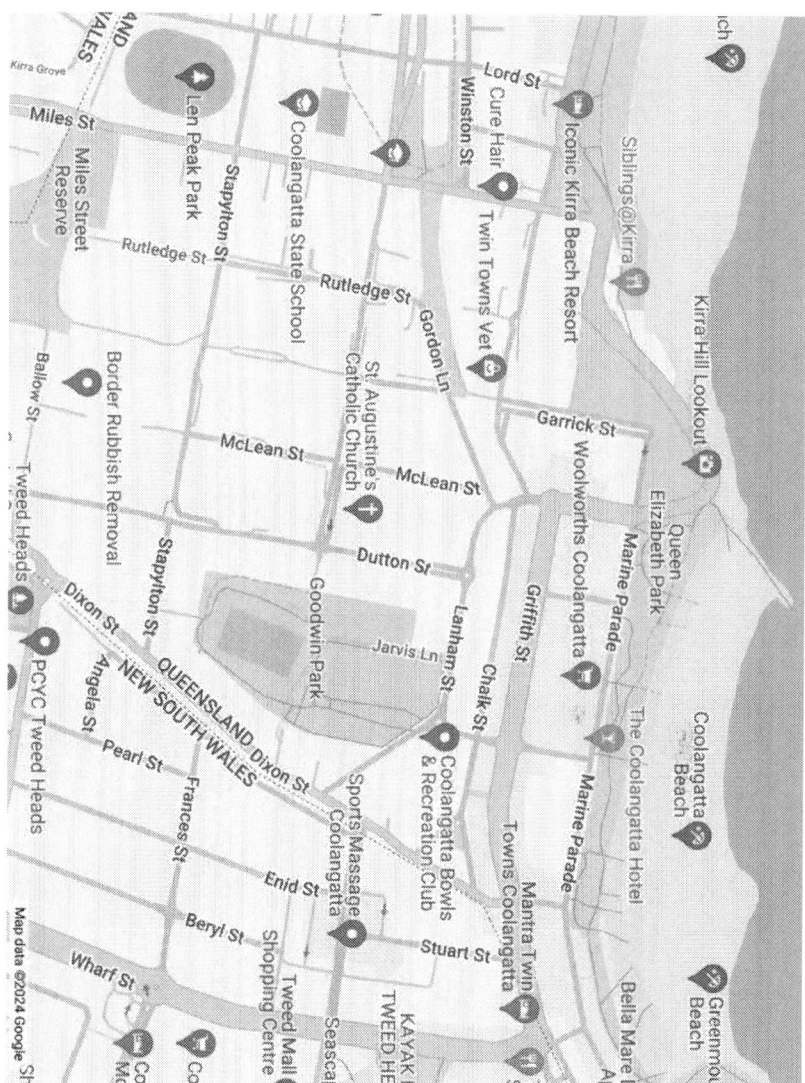

Gold Coast Travel Guide 2024 — Page 102

Map of Tamborine Mountain

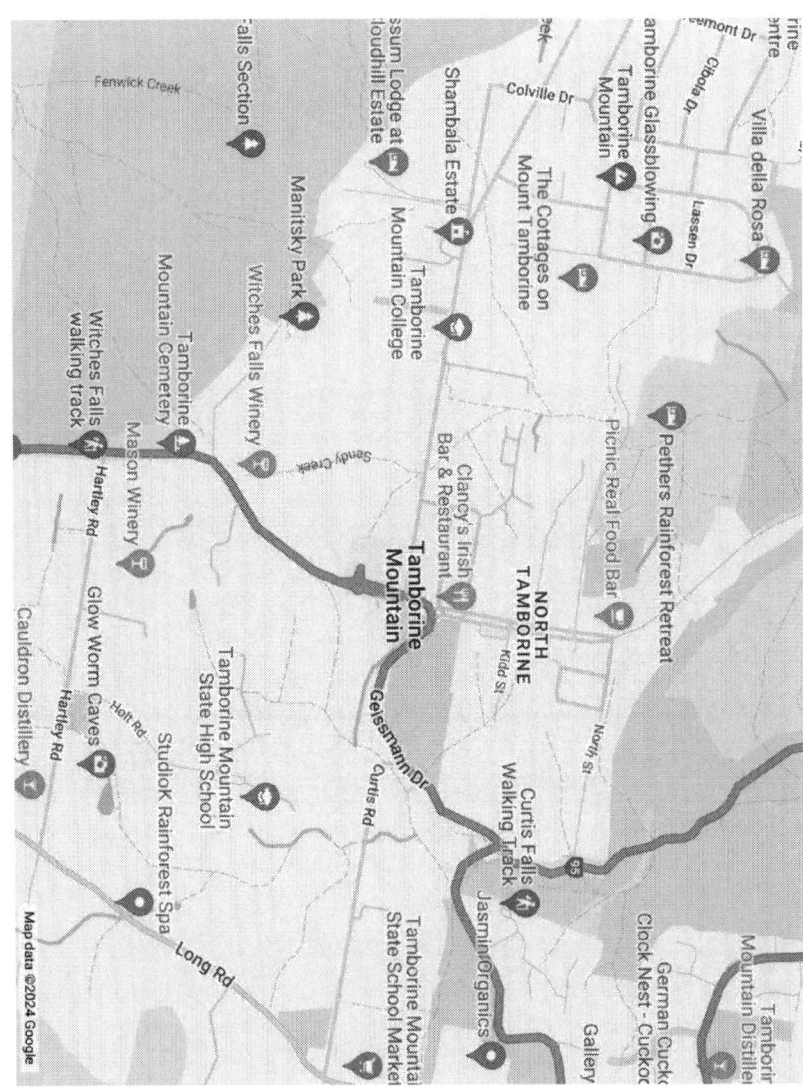

Map of Palm Beach

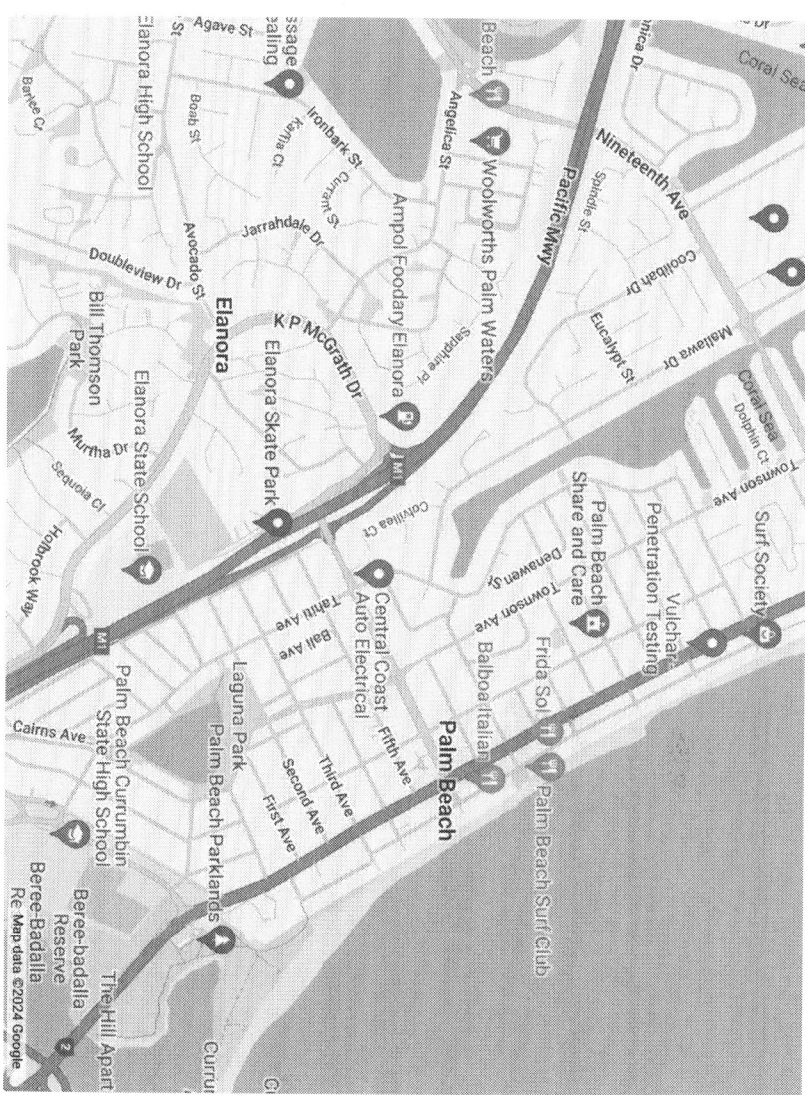

Map of Q1 Skypoint Observation Deck

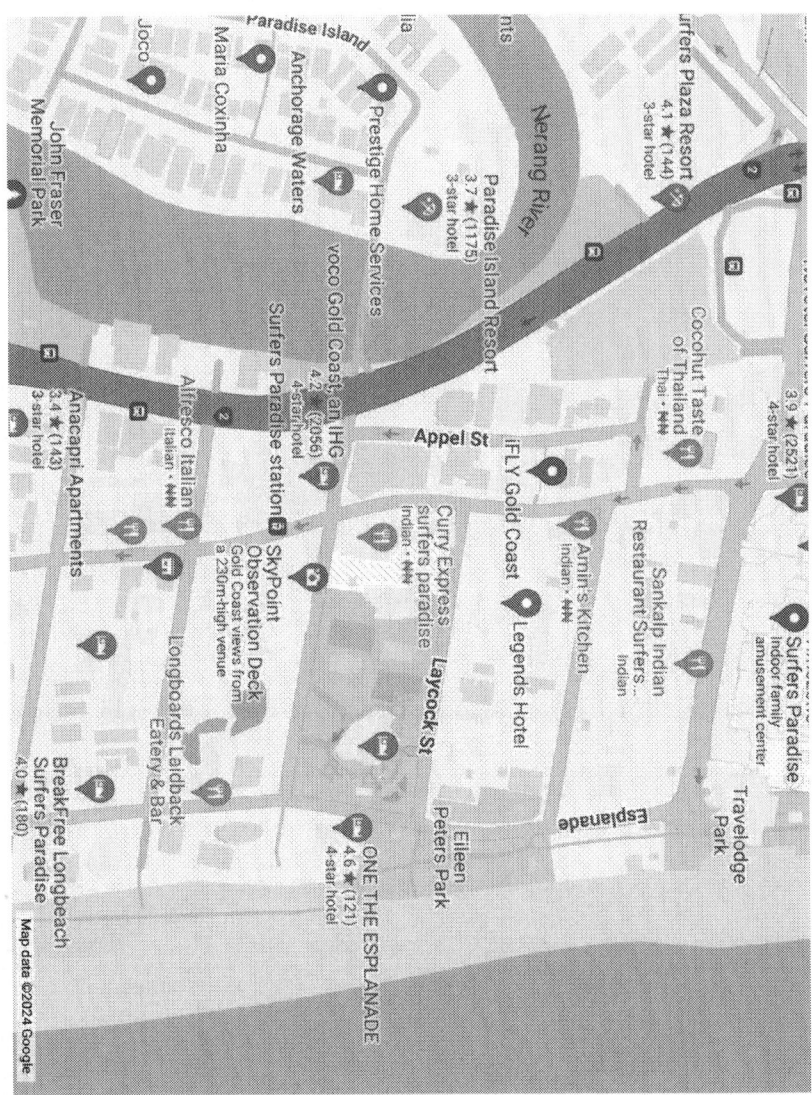

- *TransLink Transport Map:* Access the TransLink public transport map for an overview of bus and tram routes, making it easy to navigate the city.

2. Useful Contacts:

- *Emergency Services:*

    - Police, Fire, Ambulance: 000 (Emergency)

    - Non-emergency Police Assistance: 131 444

- *Health and Medical Assistance:*

    - Gold Coast University Hospital: +61 7 5687 0000

    - After-Hours GP Helpline: 1800 022 222

- *Tourist Information:*

    - Gold Coast Tourist Information Centre: +61 7 5588 2500

- *Transportation:*

    - TransLink (Public Transport): 13 12 30

    - Gold Coast Airport: +61 7 5589 1100

- *Consulates:*

    - U.S. Consulate General Brisbane: +61 7 3224 8500

GOLD COAST

- Canadian Consulate General Brisbane: +61 7 3196 0300

- COVID-19 Hotline:

    - National Coronavirus Helpline: 1800 020 080

3. Online Resources:

- *Gold Coast Tourism Website:* Explore the official Gold Coast tourism website for comprehensive information on attractions, events, and travel tips.

- *Queensland Health Website:* Stay informed about health guidelines and updates on the Queensland Health website.

- *TransLink Website:* Access schedules, routes, and other public transport information on the TransLink website.

Having access to maps and key contacts will enhance your experience on the Gold Coast, providing the tools you need for seamless navigation and assistance when required. Whether you're exploring the city, venturing into the hinterland, or enjoying the coastline, these resources will be invaluable during your stay.

CONCLUSION

As you close the pages of the "Gold Coast Travel Guide 2024," you embark on a journey not only through the vibrant landscapes and thrilling adventures of this coastal paradise but also through the rich tapestry of its history and culture. From the golden sands that kiss the turquoise waters to the adrenaline-pumping theme park rides, from the tranquil embrace of nature to the pulsating nightlife, the Gold Coast unfolds its treasures for every traveler.

As you craft your own adventure through the chapters of this guide, you'll find yourself drawn into the heart of the Gold Coast, where every moment is an opportunity for discovery and delight. Whether you're seeking the rush of extreme sports, the serenity of a rainforest hike, or the flavors of local cuisine, this guide serves as your compass, guiding you through each experience with insider tips and local insights.

But beyond the attractions and activities lies a deeper immersion into the essence of the Gold Coast – its people, its traditions, and its soul. As you delve into its cultural offerings, from museums to festivals, you'll forge connections that transcend mere sightseeing, leaving you with memories that linger long after your journey ends.

And as you bid farewell to the Gold Coast, armed with practical tips and a toolkit of resources, know that your adventure has only just begun. For the spirit of this coastal gem, with its endless possibilities and warm hospitality, will beckon you back time and again, inviting you to explore, to experience, and to embrace all that it has to offer. So, until we meet again on the shores of the Gold Coast, may your travels be filled with wonder, discovery, and endless golden moments.

To serve you better, your honest feedback is highly appreciated.

With love from Betty Vanslyke

MyJournal

Title: _____ Date: _____

MyJournal

Title: _____   Date: _____

GOLD COAST

MyJournal

Title: _____   Date: _____

MyJournal

Title: _____   Date: _____

MyJournal

Title: _____   Date: _____

MyJournal

Title: _____   Date: _____

_____
_____
_____
_____
_____
_____
_____
_____
_____
_____
_____
_____
_____
_____
_____
_____
_____
_____
_____
_____
_____
_____
_____
_____

MyJournal

Title: _____ Date: _____

MyJournal

Title: _____   Date: _____

GOLD COAST

MyJournal

Title: _____   Date: _____

MyJournal

Title: _____   Date: _____

MyJournal

Title: _____ Date: _____

MyJournal

Title: _____   Date: _____

Printed in Great Britain
by Amazon